HOW TO DEAL WITH GRIEF

MANUAL FOR COPING WITH DEATH, TRAUMA AND TRAGEDIES

KELLY ANN LEWIS

4

INTRODUCTION.

Losing someone you're keen on is often like losing one half of yourself. The pain and emptiness felt during the grieving process can continue for months or years; however no two people will ever answer an equivalent situation within the same way. Working through grief may be a day by day, week by week process. You'll have bad days once you think you'll never get over this loss. You'll also think that you simply will never function successfully without this person in your life. The great news is that you simply will recover and you'll be fully functional, if you select to.

Each and each one among us changes in various ways after the death of somebody we love.

Some of us may harden after the experience; some will soften, but those that prefer to learn and grow from this tragic time, will continue with their life remembering 'what was' and appreciating 'what is'.

Learning about grief is useful to the grieving process. In this book, we'll explore the common reactions of these experiencing a loss, alongside watching strategies for coping, assisting others who are grieving and facing the times ahead.

CHAPTER ONE.

REACTIONS TO GRIEF.

Grief may be a natural response to loss. It's the emotional suffering you are feeling when something or someone you're keen on is gone. You'll associate grief with the death of a beloved – and this sort of loss does often cause the foremost intense grief. The impact of grief can cause tremendous chaos to all or any aspects of our life. We all respond differently to grief but the foremost important thing to recollect is that the majority reactions are normal. Sometimes we discover these responses overwhelming but knowing they're normal helps us to get to terms with the changes. It's also important to notice that there's no fixed timetable for these reactions. In fact if general functioning is inhibited by any or a number of these responses, you ought to seek medical advice. Below are some common reactions to grief;

- Change in appetite

- Tightness in chest

- Headaches

- Fatigue and lack of energy

- Nausea, diarrhea, indigestion

- General aches

- Behavioral

- Sleeplessness

- Lack of motivation

- Crying (often unexpectedly)

- Social withdrawal

- Hyperactivity

- Reckless behavior (e.g. drinking]

- Shock, numbness, disbelief

- Self-blame, guilt

- Depression

- Anger

- Anxiety, panic

- Loneliness

- Relief or Indifference

- Fear

- Poor concentration

- Pre-occupation with the loss

- Seeing or hearing the person

- Dreams of the one that died

- Anger toward God

- Consolation by belief in God

- Seeking meaning of loss

- Examining meaning of life

Losing someone or something you're fond of is extremely painful. After a big loss, you'll experience all types of inauspicious and surprising emotions, like shock, anger, and guilt. Sometimes it's going to feel like the sadness will never lull. While these feelings are often frightening and overwhelming, they're normal reactions to loss. Accepting them as a part of the grieving process and allowing yourself to feel what you are feeling is important for healing. There's no right or wrong thanks to grieve — but there are healthy ways to deal with the pain. You'll get through it! Grief that's expressed and experienced features a potential for healing that eventually can strengthen and improve life.

CHAPTER TWO.

STAGES OF GRIEF.

As complicated as it feels, grief may be a process which may be worked through.

The five stages of grief:

Denial.

Immediately after the death of your beloved, you'll experience shock or denial.

This is especially noticeable if the death is sudden or unexpected or the results of an extended illness where the death wasn't foreseen. You'll only absorb small amounts of data consistent with what you'll handle. You'll awaken within the morning eager to push aside the truth of the loss and believe only what you select to simply accept.

This is an absolutely normal reaction except where the denial extends beyond a feasible time.

Anger.

When the complete impact of the loss hits home, many folks feel anger. This is often a result of having accepted the truth of the loss but yearnings for the beloved emerge. This anger is often directed to the dead person for deserting or abandoning us or displaced incorrectly to others including people that offer support, doctors and hospital staff or maybe God. At this point there's an urgent need to discuss these feelings.

Bargaining.

Bargaining is that negotiation stage and is typically when one bargains with a better being or God. We unconsciously or consciously say things like "if you're taking this pain away, I will be able to attempt to get my act together".

Depression.
Eventually the complete impact of the loss will catch up with you. Whether it's a gradual or sudden realization, you'll see that things can't be undone or changed. You'll need to come to terms with the facts and those facts are often be the reason for extreme sadness and depression. Depression should be carefully observed and addressed by professionals if needed.

Acceptance.
The final stage is that of acceptance. Gradually, we recognize that we are getting more curious about what's happening around us and start to enjoy what life has got to offer. True acceptance comes when

functioning has returned and having accepted the loss in its entirety. This is often achieved once you are ready to reminisce on yesterday together with your beloved, but are ready to enjoy today and anticipate to tomorrow.

If you're experiencing any of those emotions following a loss, it's going to help to understand that your reaction is natural which you'll heal in time. However, not everyone who is grieving goes through all of those stages – and that's okay. Contrary to popular belief, you do not need to undergo each stage so as to heal. In fact, some people resolve their grief without experiencing any of those stages. And if you are do undergo these stages of grief, you almost certainly won't experience them during a neat, sequential order, so don't worry about what you "should" be feeling or which stage you're assumed to be in.

CHAPTER THREE.

COPING WITH A LOSS.

Whether the loss of your beloved was sudden or expected, the grief related to the loss hurts. Sometimes we put ourselves through unnecessary pain by wishing for things sort of a better relationship or longer with the deceased, or the chance to mention things we didn't say once we were with the person. This is often particularly common where sudden and unexpected deaths occur. The important thing to recollect is that our beloved loved us for who we are and therefore the person we were within the relationship. Listed below are a couple of tips that help people deal with grief;

Get support.
The single most vital think about healing from loss is experiencing the support of people. Albeit you aren't comfortable talking about your feelings under normal circumstances, it's important to communicate them when you're grieving. Sharing your loss makes the burden of grief easier to hold. Wherever the support arrives from, accept it and don't grieve alone. Connecting to others will assist you heal. Address friends and relations – now's the time to rest on the people that care

about you, albeit you're taking pride in being strong and self-sufficient. Draw loved ones close, instead of avoiding them, and accept the help that's offered. Oftentimes, people want to assist but don't have an idea, so tell them what you would like – whether it's a shoulder to cry on or help with funeral arrangements.

Draw comfort from your faith.
If you're a follower of a spiritual tradition, embrace the comfort its mourning customs can provide.

Spiritual activities that are meaningful to you – like praying, meditating, or getting to church – offers solace. If you're questioning your faith within the wake of the loss, ask a clergy member or others in your religious community.

Talk to a therapist or grief counselor.
If your grief seems like it is excessive, call a psychological health professional experienced in grief counseling. An experienced therapist can assist you run through intense emotions and overcome obstacles to your grieving.

Take care of yourself.
When you're grieving, it's more important than ever to look after yourself. The strain of a serious loss can quickly deplete your energy and emotional reserves. Taking care

of your physical and emotional needs will assist you get through this difficult time.

Face your feelings.

You can attempt to suppress your grief, but you can't avoid it forever. So, to heal, you've got to acknowledge the pain. Trying to avoid feelings of sorrow and loss only extends the grieving process. Unresolved grief also can cause complications like depression, anxiety, drug abuse, and health problems.

Express your feelings during a tangible or creative way.

Write about your tragedy in a journal. If you've lost a beloved, write a letter saying the items you never had the chance to say;

make a memorabilia or photo album celebrating the person's life; or become involved in a cause or organization that was very important to him or her.

Look after your physical health.
The mind and body are connected. Once you feel good physically, you'll also feel better emotionally. Battle stress and fatigue by getting enough sleep, eating healthy, and exercising. Avoid the use of alcohol or drugs to desensitize the pain of grief or lift your mood artificially.

Don't let anyone tell you ways to feel, and don't tell yourself the way to feel either.
Your grief is your own, and nobody else can tell you when it's time to "move on" or "get

over it." Let yourself feel whatever you are feeling without embarrassment or judgment. It's acceptable to be angry, to scream at the heavens, to fight tears or not. It's also okay to laugh, to seek out moments of joy, and to part with when you're ready.

Plan ahead for grief "triggers".
Anniversaries, vacations, ceremonies and milestones can resurrect memories and feelings. Be prepared for an emotional attack, and know that it's completely normal. If you're sharing a vacation or lifecycle event with other relatives, ask them before time about their expectations

and agree on strategies to honor the person you adored.

Journal writing.

You can begin writing a journal of your feelings and emotions. Writing is one among the foremost common therapeutic tools used because it helps to dispose of unwanted feelings. Many of us enjoy journal writing as a therapeutic and healing tool when grieving.

Writing our feelings doesn't always come easy; however, once you begin you'll soon learn the advantages of getting words down and completely out of your system. Your journals are often techniques of letting out your feelings throughout this sad time, or it is often a method of saying stuff you wished you had said to the deceased. Whenever you identify feelings like anger, fear or sadness, get your journal and write. After each entry, your feelings will have a lesser impact on your lifestyle. For instance, if you're feeling angry and are ready to write on that anger and what made you angry within the first place, you're less likely to behave angrily toward those that don't understand the genesis of the anger or deserve that anger.

CHAPTER FOUR.

CUSTOMS.

There are several customs that provide us with opportunities to engage in behaviors that connect us with people we love, despite their absence. They're specifically designed actions, either physical or mental, which are used individually and supply inner peace from what was causing us pain.

Certain days are often particularly painful after the death of a beloved. These include birthdays, Christmas, anniversaries, Valentine's Day and the death anniversary itself. Confronting these events, instead of avoiding them, is that the best process to handle them.

Customs don't only acknowledge the day, but reconnect us with our beloved with fond memories and symbolic connections. When planning, concentrate on particularly significant places, events and things which meant an excellent deal to the deceased and yourself. Below may be a list of ideas for customs which you'll wish to use.

• Place a flower or tree in memory of your departed

• look around photo albums regularly

• Light a specific candle in memory of your beloved

• Wear an item of clothing / jewelry that your beloved bought for you

• Enjoy a meal which was your loved one's favorite

• Have lunch or dinner with friends at your loved one's favorite restaurant

- Read and re-read cards given to you by your beloved

- Read poetry which reminds you of your beloved

- visit places you've got been to together

- Watch movies that you simply enjoyed together

- Toast your beloved on anniversaries and birthdays

- Play music that your beloved enjoyed

- Wear perfume that your beloved liked you to wear

CHAPTER FIVE.

Helping Children Grieve.

You may not be grieving for your beloved alone. You'll have a little child or children who are grieving, and alongside your own grief, you would like to be supportive and understanding of their reactions to the death of their special someone. This chapter is for parents of youngsters who are grieving.

Children, like adults, experience grief in many various ways and every child has his or her own pace of recovery. It's impossible to predict how a toddler will answer losing a loved one; however there are certain reactions that are common to children also as adults. For instance, whilst an adult may express anger verbally, a toddler may do so through drawing pictures. Children also grieve irregularly – one minute they're crying loudly and therefore the next they're happy outside having fun with friends. Understanding the concept of loss depends on the age of the kid. Bear in mind that other factors play a role during a child's grieving, for instance, intelligence, family environment and former experience with death.

Annoyance, sobbing, searching, lack of appetite and eventually quiet resignation is that way in which a toddler will usually grieve.

What we do is way more important that what we are saying to a toddler this age. Generally, a grieving child needs large doses of tender, loving care ... holding, hugging and patting.

CHAPTER SIX.

Abnormal Grief.

Sometimes, the traditional mourning process can transform to complicated or abnormal grieving for variety of reasons. These can include the circumstances of the death, the person's history of grieving experiences, and therefore the personality of the bereaved and the availability of support.

When grief doesn't go.

It's typical to feel sad, numb, or angry following a loss. But as time passes, these emotions should subside and be less intense as you accept the loss and begin to maneuver forward. If you aren't feeling better over time, or your grief is getting worse, it's going to be a symbol that your grief has developed into a more significant issue, like complicated grief or major depression.

Complicated grief.

The sadness of losing someone you adore never goes away completely, but it shouldn't remain center stage. If the pain of the loss is so constant and severe that it keeps you from resuming your life, you'll be affected by a condition referred to as complicated grief. Complicated grief is like being plunged in a severe state of mourning. You'll have difficulties accepting the death long after it's occurred or be so immersed with the one that died that it disrupts your daily routine and sabotages your other relationships.

Symptoms of complicated grief include:

- Intense longing and looking for the deceased

- Intrusive thoughts or images of your beloved

- Denial of the death or sense of incredulity

- Imagining that your beloved is alive

- Searching for the person in familiar places

- Avoiding things that remind you of your beloved

- Extreme anger or bitterness over the loss

- Feeling that life is empty or meaningless

- The difference between grief and depression

Discerning between grief and clinical depression isn't always easy, since they share so many symptoms.

However, there are ways to discern the difference. Remember, grief may be a roller coaster. It involves a good sort of emotions and a mixture of excellent and bad days. Even when you're in the thick of the grieving process, you'll have moments of delight or happiness.

With depression, on the opposite hand, the emotions of emptiness and despair are constant. If you recognize any of the above symptoms of complicated grief or clinical depression, ask a psychological health professional directly. Left untreated, complicated grief and depression can cause remarkable emotional damage, life threatening health problems, and even suicide. But treatment can assist with your recovery.

CONCLUSION.

Together we've checked out individual reactions and feelings after the death of your beloved. We've then explored ways of coping which range from journal writing to customs. Then we've learnt the way to assist children who are grieving. And lastly, we've identified abnormal grief reactions so as to spot when our grief goes beyond what's considered normal and transcends to depression.

Many people find that after recovering from the loss of a beloved, they notice a desire to assist others. This will be achieved by doing volunteer work or assisting charities within the area of illness that affected your beloved. Others find that they move forward by setting small goals like going for a walk and taking over a craft or hobby.

There are not any short cuts to working through grief. It's a difficult process which is individual to every one of us. We'd like to figure through grief in our own time, and manage the loss of our beloved in healthy and not destructive ways. If you or someone in your family needs support, get it. Grief is often a really lonely journey if travelling it alone.

One thing to recollect after losing a beloved is that death doesn't end the connection.

It's important to acknowledge the ways in which he or she remains with you and honor these connections as you progress forward to full recovery.

As you look to the longer term, choose new goals, hopes and dreams. Prefer to start your journey of life with renewed passion as a result of having known your special person. Your life may never be one and the same now that he or she is gone, but you're an infinitely better person for having known them and richer for having been loved by them.

Made in the USA
Monee, IL
23 September 2023

43254650R00024